# The Cabin in the Hills

Story by Annette Smith

Illustrations by Mark Wilson

Dad stopped the car
at the end of the road.
"There's the path," he said.
"We will have to hurry.
It's getting dark,
and we have to get
to the cabin."

Ben and Mitch
took their bags and the flashlight
and raced on ahead,
up the path.

"It's my turn to have the top bunk," Mitch called to Ben. "You had it last time."

3

Ben got to the cabin first
and opened the door.
It was very dark inside.
He ran back
to help Mitch with his bags.

4

They ran up the steps to the cabin.
Ben heard something move.

"Don't go in, Mitch," he said.
"Stand back!
There's something inside,
and it's moving about."

"Shut the door!" shouted Mitch.
"Dad!   Dad!
There's something in the cabin."

"I'll have a look," said Dad.
"Give me the flashlight, Ben."

Dad opened the door slowly
and went into the cabin.
He shined the flashlight
up and down,
and then he saw
two big shining eyes!

7

"It's a possum!" called Dad.

The possum raced past Dad and
climbed up onto the top bunk.
Dad shined the flashlight
so that they could all see it.

"The possum thinks it has climbed up a tree," said Ben.

"We can't catch it," said Mom. "Possums move fast, and they have very sharp claws."

"We could make a noise
to scare it," said Ben.

"We can make loud clapping noises
like this," said Mitch.
"That will scare it."

Mitch and Ben
began to clap loudly,
and Dad shined the light
on the top bunk.

The possum didn't like
the loud clapping noises.
It ran down the side of the bunk,
past Mom and the boys,
and out the open door.

"It won't come back," said Mom.
"It will be way up a tree by now."

"Get your sleeping bags ready,"
said Dad.
"It's past your bedtime."

"Do you still want to sleep
on the top bunk, Mitch?"
laughed Ben.

"You mean the possum bunk?"
said Mitch.
"Yes, I'm going up
on the possum bunk.
It's my turn!"

15

"But I think I'll shut the door," said Mitch.